Third Eye Awakening

How to easily open the third eye, develop psychic power and ability, and understand the power of the pineal gland!

Table Of Contents

Introduction 1
Free Bonus 2
Chapter 1: What is the Third Eye? 3
Chapter 2: Third Eye Awakening: Health and Diet 5
Chapter 3: Third Eye Awakening: Meditation 7
Chapter 4: Third Eye Awakening: Practices 10
Chapter 5: Symptoms of Opening the Third Eye 14
Chapter 6: Causes of Third Eye Awakening 19
Chapter 7: Developing Psychic Power and Ability 21
Chapter 8: Pineal Gland & DMT 23
Chapter 9: How to avoid Pineal Gland Calcification 28
Chapter 11: The Third Eye & Brainwave Levels 45
Conclusion 51

Introduction

As human beings, it is natural for us to be curious of many different things. Because of this, we aspire to know more, and to discover new things. As much as we can, we try to explore things that are of our interests.

The third eye – its existence, and the whole truth about it, has been a debate for many people. For a long time now, people have argued about whether or not a sixth sense really exists, and if it does, how people can activate it. Whether or not awakening the third eye is a good thing, people are still curious about it, and are willing to take risks to discover what exists beyond what our naked eye can see.

To help you with questions about the third eye, developing psychic abilities, and how to awaken it, this book is for you. It provides historical information regarding different cultures beliefs on the third eye. You will discover what the third eye can be used for, the different theories surrounding it, and how to activate and awaken your own third eye.

This book is the 2nd edition, recently updated with additional information on the Third Eye, it's functions, and how to activate and use it properly! This is now truly the complete guide to third eye awakening, and will serve you well as you begin to activate and use your third eye.

Thanks again for taking the time to read this book, I hope you enjoy it!

Free Bonus

As a thank you for taking the time to download my book, I'd like to offer you a **FREE** bonus!

I have compiled a list of my '7 Keys For Successful Meditation', and have made it free for you to download.

You can CLICK HERE to claim your free copy, or click on the link below:
http://bit.ly/1F91lfl

Meditation helps you to clear and focus your mind, and allows you to gain better control over your thoughts and focus. Regular meditation can make it a lot easier to successfully engage in things like Reiki healing, aura viewing, and opening your third eye, as these all involve deep and powerful use of your mind and focus.

So download my free report today – CLICK HERE – and begin experiencing the amazing benefits of meditation today!

Chapter 1:
What is the Third Eye?

Most likely, the concept of the Third Eye is no longer new to you. You may have heard of a friend sharing to you how amazing or terrible his or her third eye experience was. You may have watched a television show that demonstrated how the third eye works. Similarly, you may have experienced it on your own. Regardless of your experiences, or lack thereof, this chapter will introduce to you what the third eye is, and how science has explained it through the pineal gland.

The Third Eye is a concept used to refer to an invisible eye; one said to be capable of providing perception beyond what our naked eye can ordinarily see. According to some spiritual traditions, it has the ability to communicate with the past, predict the future, and allow the wielder to have an encounter with spiritual and psychological entities. The third eye is usually associated with the pineal gland. The pineal gland is an endocrine gland located in the vertebrate brain. It excretes melatonin, which is responsible for the modulation of a human's sleeping patterns. The third eye is usually equated with the pineal gland. This is because the pineal gland is located in the center of our two eyes, and is also shaped quite similarly. Although there are still no scientific studies proving that the pineal gland has such an ability, many people have long believed that it provides a sixth sense.

All human beings have a third eye, however only some people are able to activate it, while some people are not. Debates are actually still ongoing as to whether it exists or not. Some religions argue that when one encounters such kind of sense, he or she must not open it and use it, since it is not the work of God. However, for other religious traditions, opening the third eye is a healthy spiritual activity. It allows one to prepare for his or her life, since he or she has an access to what lies beyond the "normal" world.

Awakening the Third Eye is a risky decision. As some experts suggest, "Be careful what you wish for". Before attempting to do so, make sure that you prepare yourself well for the new and not necessarily pleasant things that you may experience.

The following chapters will share to you the simple, yet effective ways to awaken your third eye.

Chapter 2:
Third Eye Awakening: Health and Diet

This chapter will share to you ways that you can awaken your third eye, firstly by focusing on your health and diet. Experts on third eye awakening suggest that in order to effectively open your third eye, you should make adjustments to your health and diet as mentioned below:

1. Detoxify or Stimulate your Pineal Gland

You can do this by trying out pineal gland detoxifiers or stimulants such as chlorella, blue-green algae, D3, hydrilla verticillata, Iodine, chlorophyll, ginseng, and liver oil. When activating your third eye, it is important that your pineal gland is purified.

2. Be careful when using water – whether when drinking, cooking, or bathing.

You need to avoid getting in contact with fluoride, especially during water intake. Inorganic vegetables and fruits, artificial drinks, and red meat use unsafe and impure water in their production, and that is why you should avoid them as well. Water circulates all throughout your body, and that is why it is important to have a clean and safe intake of it. Unsafe and impure water intake may bring harm and danger to the different organs in your body, which may affect the effective opening of your third eye.

3. Include in your diet food with natural detoxifying properties.

You may have been practicing an unhealthy diet; and this is not good if you wish to open your third eye effectively. You should watch closely the kinds of food included in your diet. It will be important to take away the unhealthy ones and replace them with food that has natural detoxifying and nourishing properties. This will make it easier for you to purify your pineal gland.

4. Relax

In attempting to open your third eye, one of the most important things that you should remind yourself is to relax. Relax your mind, body and soul. This is important for meditation because you will not be able to concentrate properly if there are certain things that are bothering you. Free your mind for this moment and just let everything flow freely.

Chapter 3:
Third Eye Awakening: Meditation

The previous chapter taught you the necessary preparations you need to make in terms of your health and diet in order to purify and detoxify your pineal gland. This chapter will now teach you the preparations you need to do before meditation, and steps on how to meditate effectively in order to open your third eye. Only do this when you are one hundred percent sure that you want to awaken your third eye. The steps are as follows:

1. **Find a peaceful place to meditate.**

    It is important to look for a quiet place to meditate. It must be an environment where nothing will distract you for at least thirty minutes. This is because you will need to focus and calm your mind and body when meditating.

2. **Correct your posture.**

    When you are in a quiet and peaceful place, you should now assume a meditative posture. This can be done by sitting on flat ground with your legs crossed, your hands placed on your knees, and your back straight. You can also sit in a chair if this position is uncomfortable to you. Throughout the whole meditation, you should maintain a straight back by preventing it to slouch. Point your chest out and your keep your shoulders down.

3. **Keep your body relaxed.**

   You will not be able to focus properly if your body is tense. Before and during meditation, it is important and helpful to keep your body relaxed. Rolling your head from side to side can also help you keep the tension away. Release the tension in your muscles so you can focus properly.

4. **Keep your mind relaxed.**

   This is one of the most difficult parts of awakening your third eye because you need to release all of the thoughts in your mind. This can be extremely difficult because it takes a lot of effort to keep your mind from thinking. In one way or another, what is happening in the physical world may distract you. The technique is to focus on the exhalation and inhalation of your breath. This will require patience since it may take you a long time and plenty of practice before you can consistently keep distracting thoughts out of your mind.

5. **Make meditation a habit.**

   Meditation will be more effective when you do it often. Meditating occasionally will help you train yourself to stay focused and relaxed. You may encounter some difficulties at first, but as you practice, it will become much easier.

6. **Be observant.**

   Meditation can be more effective if your intuitive side is active. You can activate this by allowing yourself to observe the things happening around you. By observing the conversations of people, and taking notes on how they respond to particular circumstances, you will have a greater ability to interpret their behavior, especially non-verbal ways of communication. This can be your first step in reading the minds of the people around you. Try to make assumptions on what they are thinking during particular circumstances.

7. **Listen to your gut instincts.**

   Gut instincts are the peculiar feelings that you experience when you feel that something is likely to happen. Everyone has gut instincts, only some people ignore them. It is important that you take down your gut instincts and note whether they truly happen or not. This is one of the first steps in developing your psychic ability. Whenever you feel like something might take place even if you do not have enough evidence to support your claim, note it down. Do not underestimate your gut instincts, because they can turn out to be true.

8. **Keep track of your dreams.**

   Similar to gut instincts, it is also possible that your dreams correspond to particular events in real life. When you dream of something, it is also important to note it down and see if what you dreamt happens. By keeping track of your dreams, you are a step closer to unleashing your psychic power.

Now that you know the basic things you need to do before and during meditation, the next things you need to know are the chants and practices that you should perform. The next chapter will share to you how to awaken your third eye through chants and traditional practices.

Chapter 4:
Third Eye Awakening: Practices

This chapter will inform you of the steps that you should undertake when you are performing a chant to open your third eye. As experts suggest, you need to do this exercise only for three days, and after that, the changes will be permanent.

During the whole chant process, you need to remind yourself of the mantra, "Thoh". You pronounce it the same way you pronounce the word "toe". Utter this mantra with a specific tone and proper vibration, as well as a moderate pitch. To help you get the right tone for your mantra, here are some helpful tips:

1. **Maintain a proper posture.**

    Maintain the same posture that you use when you are meditating. Keeping your back straight will help you stay focused for the entire chant.

2. **Moderate your breathing.**

    Keep your breathing relaxed by paying attention to the way you inhale and exhale. Once you are already relaxed, inhale through your nose and hold it as long as you are still comfortable. Slightly part your teeth by opening your jaws, and then place your tongue in between your upper and lower teeth.

3. **Apply pressure onto your tongue.**

    As instructed in the second step, you must place your tongue in between your upper and lower teeth. Once it is already in the proper position, apply pressure onto it by exhaling slowly through your mouth while uttering the mantra in one long release of your breath. As you exhale for a couple more times, say it again once every exhalation. To check if you are doing this properly, you should feel air passing through your tongue and teeth, and you will feel a pressure on your cheeks and jaw. If you are able to do this properly, this exercise will vibrate in your third eye. If you find some difficulties, just do it again and again until you finally get it right.

4. **Do it five times.**

    Repeat the process mentioned above five times. It is important to make sure that you are doing the exercise properly.

5. **Do the exercise for three days.**

    Once you are able to do the exercise properly, do it for three days. It must be consecutive and done 24 hours apart. Once you have performed it for five times in three consecutive days, its effects will be permanent. You will have awakened your third eye.

After performing these steps properly and successfully, you have now opened your third eye. However, it does not end there. You will still have to take note of the things that you need to do two weeks after you have performed the above exercise. The steps for the second part of the awakening are as follows:

1. **Take a deep breath.**

    Hold your breath for five seconds. Repeat this three times. Similar to the first stage of awakening, this will help you relax and focus.

2. **Release your breath by vibrating the word "may".**

    Do as you have done in the first stage of awakening. After taking a deep breath, release your breath by uttering the word "may" while releasing it slowly through your mouth. Say the mantra using a moderate and vibrating tone. You can check if you are doing this properly by following the procedures stated on the first stage of awakening.

3. **Concentrate on your pineal gland.**

    As you perform these exercises, it is important that you concentrate on your third eye, or on the center of your brain. While doing the chant, put your focus on the top of your head until you finish saying the mantra.

4. **Do the exercise five times.**

    After you finish a round, do the chant four more times.

Compared to the first stage of third eye awakening, the second stage is much more pleasurable. The first stage may cause headaches and pains, while the second stage of third eye awakening gives pleasure and comfort. After doing the exercise, you will feel lightness and bliss.

Aside from the first and second stages of third eye awakening, experts have also shared some tips and techniques on how to make the awakening more effective. According to them, using quartz, gems, and crystals can also help sharpen your focus while opening your third eye. There are certain gems and crystals that have energetic vibrations, and therefore have direct connections to the pineal gland. Some of these crystals are lapis lazuli, amethyst, blue tourmaline, and blue topaz. You can put these crystals on your neck or head to make your concentration more effective.

Now that you know the steps and techniques that you can use to awaken your third eye, it is important that you know if you have successfully performed the introduced procedures. There are signs and symptoms that you will experience if you are able to do the steps properly. These signs and symptoms will help you determine if you have really awakened your third eye, or if you need to correct and improve you performances on the chants in order to effectively activate it. The next chapter will inform you of the signs and symptoms that show whether or not you are already opening your third eye.

Chapter 5:
Symptoms of Opening the Third Eye

There are signs and symptoms that should tell you whether you were successful at opening your third eye. This chapter will share the signs and symptoms to guide you in your spiritual awakening. If these signs and symptoms show, it means that you have already opened your third eye.

One of the ways in which you can see whether you are effectively opening your third eye is when you begin feeling some changes in your body. You begin to have unusual feelings on the physical, emotional, mental, and spiritual aspects of your life. You suddenly notice that there are changes in your behavior, and you respond to certain events in a way that you didn't usually do before. These changes in your patterns of behavior indicate that you are now opening your third eye. You are also more energetic than usual. This feeling of lightness that you experience is the effect of doing the second stage of third eye awakening.

One of the most common signs and symptoms of third eye awakening is experiencing headaches or head itching. When you suddenly feel that your head is aching or itching, it means that your crown chakra is starting to open. This crown chakra supposedly connects you to the spiritual and divine world, which is one of the benefits of opening your third eye. Headaches and head itching are indicators that you are now beginning to have access to spiritual entities. This may be uncomfortable for you, but just be patient and just bear with it because it will pass after some time.

Another symptom of third eye awakening is unusual sleeping patterns. You may notice that after you have performed the chants, you sleep and wake up at times when you do not usually do before. There may even be times when you will wake up at three o'clock sharp in the morning. This is said to be explained by the spiritual entities that tap you while you are asleep. Experts suggest that you should not be bothered with these things, and you should not be worried that you may be weak during the next day because of lack of sleep. As promised, you will have high levels of energy that are even comparable to having complete hours of sleep. This symptom may also trouble you, but similar to headaches and head itching, it will pass. It only means that your body is now adjusting to the awakening.

Even though you do not always get a complete and good sleep, you will dream unusual and unrealistic dreams most of the time. You may take them for granted at first because you may think that they do not mean anything, but it is important to pay attention to your dreams. They may be unrealistic as they appear, but if you analyze them more closely, you will realize that they correspond to some events in your life, and they have meanings that will help you with your life. It will be helpful to consult books and websites that talk about the meanings and interpretations of dreams so that you will know what to do.

Another common symptom of third eye awakening is ringing and buzzing. You will often hear these sounds. At times, they may be disturbing and irritating but these sounds are the divine entities that are vibrating after you have performed the rituals and chants. Do not be bothered by them. Just listen to them and acknowledge them, because they will eventually disappear. If you begin hearing these kinds of sounds, it is a sign that you have opened your third eye.

Third eye awakening is not always pleasurable. Part of the process is the feeling of ache and pains that you may experience in your entire body. You may often feel muscular tension, pain in the joints, and other parts of your body. Too much vibration may also cause you to get fatigue. This is because the body is adjusting to the chakra opening. You will also feel pain and difficulty in your chest. Sometimes, you will experience palpitations even if you do not have any medical conditions associated with it. You may feel that your heart is skipping a beat occasionally, even if you are not tired or exhausted. You may experience chest pains and you will have a feeling of heaviness in your chest. Even if you do not have medical conditions associated with heart and lung problems, you will encounter these difficulties as part of the opening of the heart chakra. Aching of the head, skull, face, eyes, and other organs will also occur. This may irritate you but as you develop your psychic ability, they will eventually disappear.

Part of the opening of the third eye is the experience of an emotional roller coaster. You will experience frequent and unusual mood changes. You may be very happy at one moment, and be very sad at another. You may feel very energetic at one moment, and be very tired at another. You will also feel nervous and anxious at times, even if there are no apparent reasons to feel so. You may have panic attacks and become overly worried even if there is nothing to worry about. Your emotions may sometimes be out of your control, but these are all part of the chakra opening process. You will also encounter times when you are talking to yourself. This is all a part of getting through your emotional roller coaster.

Another symptom is an increased appetite or craving for food. You suddenly feel that your body needs more food consumption than you usually do. This is because there is a higher level of energy required by the vibration, and in turn, your body must be able to cope with it. You will crave for particular foods most of the time and you will eat more than you usually do.

Oftentimes, you will feel the need to seclude yourself from other people. You have an increased desire to be by yourself. This is because being alone gives you more time to know yourself better. You will feel a certain feeling of detachment from your friends, family and loved ones. You may lose interest in many things and will not choose to socialize even if you always did before.

There may also be times when you experience unusual things with your cellphones and other electronic devices. For example, they turn off or suddenly do not work properly for any apparent reason. Again, the high level of energy because of your vibration is causing all of this. This phase is normal and even though it may trouble you, and scare you at times, this will pass. You should get used to these kinds of unusual experiences. All throughout the process of opening your third eye, you will encounter unusual things.

You should also be reminded that you may experience time shifts. You will feel that time is moving either too fast or too slow. You will also be encountering many instances that you think have already happened in the past. This feeling is "déjà vu". These kinds of experiences are all part of feeling distortion in time.

Lastly, you will feel an unusual and special kind of connection to the divine world. You will feel that you are so close to God or some spirit. You feel guided and loved. You will experience a lot of difficulties and emotional problems at first, but later on you will feel peace and understanding. You will want to leave this place and be with God or some spirit because you feel that it is where home is.

Mentioned above are the most common signs and symptoms that your third eye is opening. But remember, one it has been opened there is no going back.

So why do people decide to open their third eye? What are the causes of awakening? The following chapter will further discuss these questions.

Chapter 6:
Causes of Third Eye Awakening

It is important to know the things that drive a person to have his or her third eye opened. This chapter will inform you of the possible and most common reasons for third eye awakening. This will help you to understand why people decide to experience something beyond what normally exists. The most common causes of third eye awakening are as follows:

1. **Death of a loved one.** When you lose a person you love, you feel extremely sad and your mood goes down. You may even get depressed. Because of this, we look for comfort from other people or things. Some people, however, feel the need to reconnect to their spirit once a loved one dies. They seek comfort by looking at their spirituality. This brings them closer to psychic awakening.

2. **Near death experience or accidents.** Psychic experiences usually occur during near death experiences or accidents. This may sometimes be because of an encounter with a spirit that guides you and thus rescued you from that near death experience.

3. **Healing.** Experts suggest that healing requires the presence of high levels of energy, which ignites our sixth sense. Experiences with these high levels of energy can increase your vibration, and trigger the psychic awakening inside you. As energy flows through you, a shift in your awareness occurs.

Mentioned above are just some of the most common causes of third eye awakening. There may be other factors that are distinct from other people; these are unique experiences that trigger the third eye awakening, and thus, people choose to experience what is beyond the reality that is known to common people.

The next chapter will inform you of the psychic powers and abilities that you will develop once you've activated your third eye.

Chapter 7:
Developing Psychic Power and Ability

What happens to your psychic power and abilities when you have finally opened your third eye? This chapter will inform you of the developments and improvements that your psychic power and abilities will undergo after you have successfully opened your third eye. These kinds of abilities are unique, and there are only very few people capable of doing these things. It is therefore important to use these powers for good, and not to cause harm to other people.

One of the most evident effects of third eye awakening is increased ability to concentrate and make decisions. Because you have enhanced imagination and prediction of things, you will be able to make wise and correct decisions. You may sometimes see into the future clearly, and this will help you to improve your life. You will have the ability to surmise what may happen in the future, and it is likely that these assumptions will indeed occur.

Among other people, you will have the ability to experience entities that a lot of people do not encounter with in normal reality. You will encounter many different things that are apart from the kind of reality that you typically know. You will have access to the divine world, and will oftentimes experience spiritual intercessions. It is highly possible that you experience and converse with spiritual entities that are usually feared by other people. To you, however, this is a privilege.

Lastly, you will be more capable of anticipating the things that will happen. Since you can now focus better, and you have the ability to predict what happens, you will find it easier to assert your behavior during particular circumstances. You are equipped with better psychic skills and abilities.

It is a privilege to have these psychic powers and abilities, but it is important to remind ourselves that we should use them for the good and for the betterment of everyone's life.

Chapter 8:
Pineal Gland & DMT

There are many different theories and beliefs about what the third eye is, and how it works.

Hindus consider the third eye as the sixth of the seven chakras, or energy centers found at certain points along the spine. For them this third eye chakra, or Ajna chakra, is the place that connects the spiritual realm with the physical one. Ajna is translated as 'command', and this chakra is associated with intellect and intuition. Hindus often mark the third eye spot – you can find this at the middle of their forehead near the center of their eyebrows.

Taoists have a similar belief, but they call the third eye as the 'niwan' or 'the muddy pellet'. Instead of the chakras though, the Taoists believe in energy meridians, and the muddy pellet represents the brain and the seat of the spirit. The third eye is essentially the mind's eye for Taoists.

Theosophists consider the third eye as the pineal gland. They believe that the pineal gland used to be an eye located at the back of the head of ancient humans, but it eventually shrunk deep within the brain. This information is said to be channeled by Helena Blavatsky, the co-founder of the Theosophist Society.

The ancient Egyptians may also be referring to the third eye when they designed the eye of Horus symbol. Some have noticed striking similarities between this symbol and some brain parts: the symbol's eyebrow is the corpus callosum, the eye is the thalamus, the long line beside the eye is the pineal gland, the stalk is the hypothalamus, and the curvy part is the medulla oblongata. However, we don't actually know whether they attributed mystical powers to this gland, especially because they routinely threw away the brain before turning their dead into mummies.

Some people have also linked Bible scriptures to the third eye. Matthew 6:22, which reads, "The light of the body is the eye: if therefore thine eye be single, thy whole body shall be full of light," is said to be a reference to this elusive organ. Genesis 32:22-31 narrated Jacob's encounter with God at the place called 'Peniel' or 'face of God.' Penial and pineal are similar so some think they are meaningfully related.

In relatively more recent times, 17th century philosopher Rene Descartes surmised that the pineal gland is the physical organ where the soul resides. He pointed out that since we have two eyes and two ears yet we see and hear singular visions and sounds, and since we think one thought at a time, we must have a singular organ that processes them. He chose the pineal gland because it is located at the center of the head and is the likely convergence point of our thoughts and perceptions. According to him, this gland makes it possible for the soul to reflect on what happens to the body and control its movements.

The New Age movement has popularized the third eye for many things: as a tool to gain psychic abilities, a means for attaining higher consciousness, and a link to God or the divine. Third eye exercises usually involve empowering psychic abilities and/or attaining spiritual enlightenment.

To cut the long story short, the third eye is associated with the following things:

- Psychic experiences
- Extraordinary perception
- The mind's eye
- The place that links the spiritual and the physical
- An enlightened state of mind
- The pineal gland

Although these may seem to be different things at first, they basically mean the same thing: we have a tool (whether physical or immaterial) that we can develop to achieve things that we normally could not do.

The Pineal gland and DMT

As mentioned above, some believe that the third eye is the pineal gland. To elaborate on that, the pineal gland has particular features that may be connected with a third eye of sorts:

Interestingly, the pineal gland may indeed be an old eye that has atrophied over the ages. The pineal glands of humans and animals alike are sensitive to light. These receive signals from the eyes through the optic nerves. Mainstream science explains that the pineal gland is light-sensitive because it estimates the time of day to regulate biological processes in the body.

This gland produces hormones such as melatonin and serotonin – two hormones that are important for various bodily functions. Melatonin in particular is released when it is dark, because this is the time when the person is supposed to be sleeping. Melatonin repairs damaged cells during sleep, when tissue repair is most effective.

Although it's common knowledge that we see from our two eyes, it's possible that this third eye allows us to see beyond the physical. It may be that the images we see in our head are seen by our internal eye.

Aside from being eye-like, the pineal gland produces a vision-inducing substance called DMT (dimethyltryptamine). Dr. Rick Strassman, a DMT researcher, says that DMT may be produced by the pineal gland and it may be responsible for producing dreams, visions and mystical experiences. DMT is indeed found in the pineal glands of rats, but more studies need to be made to confirm whether the pineal gland does create DMT. Trace amounts can be found in human blood, urine, cerebrospinal fluid, and organ tissues though.

DMT is known to cause hallucinations in the people who take them. Dr. Strassman has conducted experiments with volunteers who took doses of DMT. They reported to have intense visions – some describe it as an alien world while others call it a parallel universe. They met beings while in this realm, and it's interesting to note that they sometimes came back with information that they did not have prior to their DMT session.

Outside the laboratory setting, people have taken DMT from plants such as peyote and ayahuasca. Shamans have used these plants for a long time. Nowadays, they are guiding non-shamans in taking DMT-infused plants to assist them in spiritual journeys. If you are interested in these guided experiences, they are traditionally available in Peru, but are slowly becoming available in Western countries also. However, be careful, because taking high dosages of DMT will make you experience bizarre things and may be physically distressing for you.

Aside from serving as an eye, the pineal gland may be a transmitter and a signal transducer as well. It was discovered that the pineal gland contains zirconium diamonds – a material that can be used to build radios. Birds use this substance as a biological GPS to help them navigate. Zirconium diamond has a property called piezoelectricity – this allows it to translate vibrations into electricity and vice versa. This feature may allow the pineal gland to serve as the intermediary between subjective experience and objective reality. In metaphysical language, the pineal gland may translate frequencies emanating from the various realms into something we can comprehend. It serves as our radio to send and receive information through extraordinary means.

In conclusion, the pineal gland is said to be the physical third eye itself because of its eye-like properties and its vision-inducing DMT. Taking care of this gland may enable one to 'awaken' his/her third eye and perceive beyond what he/she ordinarily perceives.

Chapter 9:
How to avoid Pineal Gland Calcification

Have you ever noticed that children can sometimes see what you don't? You can blame their active imaginations for this, but it's possible that they are seeing something from their third eye. Children are said to be more in touch with their psychic abilities because their pineal glands are not calcified yet.

The pineal gland has a water-filled interior. It can get calcified as the person ages. Being calcified means being hardened by calcium salts – which is not good for the pineal gland.

You need to decalcify the pineal gland to make it function better. These are the things that calcify the gland.

- Fluoride – Fluoride is toxic to the pineal gland. This is found in fluoridated toothpaste, food and water.

- Processed food – Processing food sometimes causes it to become infused with fluoride.

- Calcium supplements – Excess calcium that is not absorbed by the body will be distributed in the blood and end up in your pineal gland.

- Lack of sunlight – Sunlight stimulates the pineal gland.

- Lack of sleep – Anything that throws off your body clock will also be stressful for your pineal gland. Melatonin (a substance released at night) is said to be converted into DMT in the pineal gland. This is one thing that gives the pineal gland its 'powers'.

- Disempowering beliefs – Your thoughts literally affect the wiring of your brain. If you have beliefs that prevent you from accessing your pineal gland abilities, your mind will indeed work in a way that will prevent the pineal gland from functioning as well as it should.

Here are some things you can do to help your pineal gland work more effectively:

Reduce fluoride intake: You can take in fluoride through eating, drinking, or absorbing it through your skin.

This means avoiding fluoridated toothpaste and dental treatments. There are toothpastes that do not contain fluoride; use them instead.

Drink non-fluoridated water. Tap water usually contains fluoride so it's best to treat your water further before drinking. Reverse osmosis, distillation filtration, and activated alumina defluoridation filtration remove fluoride from water. Boiling, freezing, and using ordinary filters does not always remove fluoride effectively. Check bottled water and beverages to see if they contain fluoride.

Avoid processed food if possible. This may contain small amounts of fluoride. Mechanically deboned meat may contain fluoride from bones. Canned food and preserves may contain fluoride because it is a commonly used preservative.

Before eating something, check whether fluoride is indicated on the label.

Avoid consuming red or black rock salt. These have fluoride minerals.

Avoid drinking red or black tea. These contain a lot of fluoride.

Avoid processed beverages. Drink natural juice from organic fruits instead.

Select organic vegetables and fruits. These are likely to contain little to no amounts of fluoride pesticides.

When cooking, avoid using non-stick pans. These are composed of fluorine compounds.

Find out whether your medication or medical treatment includes fluoride. Ask your doctor for fluoride-free alternatives.

Install fluoride filters over faucets and showers. If showering, limit your shower time to avoid absorbing excessive fluorine. Do not soak yourself in the bathtub if you do not have a filter.

Avoid calcium supplementation: This accumulates in your body and is absorbed by the pineal gland. Do not take more calcium than what you need.

Expose yourself to some sunlight: Go out when the sunlight is not yet too harsh. Gaze at sunlight (not the sun) for at least 5 minutes. Some people practice 'sun gazing' or staring directly at the sun. You <u>don't</u> have to do this! Take care of your eyes!

Sleep when it's dark: Melatonin production starts during the evening hours (around 7 pm), peaks at midnight, and stops around sunrise. Maximize the availability of melatonin by sleeping during these hours.

Detoxifications: Detoxifying diets cleanse your body of impurities. These may also be helpful for clearing out your pineal gland and reducing the toxins that may accumulate in it. Before trying a diet however, it's best to consult a doctor to determine whether or not it's safe for you personally.

Engage in spiritual practice: Spiritual activities exercise your pineal gland's function of connecting to the spiritual realms. This can be something as simple as praying or as elaborate as conducting full-blown rituals.

Meditate: Meditation enables the person to achieve states of mind that allow the third eye to function at its best.

There are meditative techniques that are designed specifically for third eye activation, such as:

- Humming: The pineal gland is said to respond to vibrations because it has a piezoelectric nature. Sit comfortably on a chair or on the floor with your back straight. Close your eyes – this will help you focus your awareness on your inner eye. Inhale deeply and slowly. Exhale and at the same time make an 'hmmm' or 'om' sound with your mouth closed. Allow your lips to vibrate. Let this sensation travel across your cheeks, to your temples, forehead, and into the third eye. Do this for as long as you can.

- Intend for your third eye to heal. You can imagine your third eye chakra or pineal gland becoming stronger and healthier. You can visualize healing light entering your forehead to cleanse your third eye chakra. Do this for as long as you want – the strength of your desire and your belief in the meditation will matter more than the length of time you do it or even the steps that you take.

- Placing awareness in the third eye. Awareness is a form of energy. It also represents your soul. You energize your third eye by focusing on it. Locate it with your mind. Observe how it feels. Notice as much as you can about it. This will concentrate your mental energy into the area and activate it.

- Kundalini yoga. Kundalini yoga is a complicated technique in itself so you may need to find a class or teacher for this. Basically, it involves the awakening of the 'kundalini' which is coiled at the bottom of the spine. When it is awakened, it is said to pierce through the chakras and rise to the top of the skull. When this happens, you will be connected with the divine and gain spiritual abilities.

Develop your Third Eye Chakra: There is an entire practice on developing the body's chakras. Chakra development is ideally done from the bottom chakra upwards because a lower chakra serves as a springboard for the one above it. Nonetheless, you can skip this process for as long as you want, given that you do your best to meditate and live a balanced life.

Life force circulates throughout the body through channels. The main channel lies along the spine where the chakras are found. These chakras are energy centers – these have roles in various aspects of our lives – for example, the root chakra deals with survival, the solar plexus chakra manages personal power, etc. As mentioned before, the third eye chakra serves as the link between the physical and non-physical worlds. It affects our state of mind and our psychic abilities.

The states of our chakras affect our experiences, and our experiences likewise affect our chakras. Healthy chakras enable us to perform well in life. Negative emotions, repressions, obsessions, and problems can taint the quality and movement of the energies within the chakras.

The signs of an unbalanced third eye chakra are the following: confusion, stagnation, aimlessness, an inability to access psychic faculties, attachment to material things, superficiality, lack of vision, learning and vision problems, headaches, and other illnesses related to the head area.

A balanced third eye chakra leads to clear thinking, strong psychic skills, attunement to the spiritual realms, a comprehension of the bigger picture, a healthy detachment from materialism, wisdom, and a healthy brain, eyes, and mind.

Visualize light/energy going into the third eye: The chakras are associated with elements – the third eye chakra's element is light. Energize it by imagining light (preferably indigo-colored as it is the chakra's color) streaming into your forehead.

Use crystals: Crystals and gemstones are sometimes used to achieve certain goals such as to feel more secure, to accept love, to gain courage, etc. Some stones are associated with the 7 chakras, and using them is said to strengthen the chakras that are assigned to them. Lapis lazuli, sodalite, sapphire, amethyst, and other indigo-colored crystals and stones are said to work well with the third eye. You can hold an indigo stone in your hand while meditating, or carry it in a pocket or pouch. You can also place the stone against your forehead, or look at it while imagining that you're absorbing its energies.

Affirmations: Affirmations are instructions that program your mind, and they can manifest in reality as well via the law of attraction. These are some examples of affirmations to empower your third eye.

- "I am one with the universe"
- "I open myself to the infinite"
- "I am ready to receive intuitive guidance"
- "I am thinking well and seeing clearly"
- "I am becoming more and more aware of spiritual realms"

You can create your own affirmations for third eye development. Just make sure that the affirmations give you a positive feeling when you say them. They should not leave you frustrated that it will never happen. To work around doubts, you can construct your affirmations as a choice. For example, "I choose to believe that I am capable of awakening my third eye." Say these affirmations as often as you can while in a receptive state of mind.

Have a dream journal: Dreams are within the domain of the third eye. Recording your dreams will train your mind into remembering them instead of discarding them as soon as you wake up. It will also strengthen your ability to control your dreams. Keep your journal beside you, and write down your dream upon awakening. If you asked a question before sleeping, or if you were ruminating on a problem, the solution might come up in a dream.

Be aware of synchronicities: Synchronicities are separate events that can be meaningfully related to each other. Although the connections may seem illogical, they are said to be a result of the interconnection of everything at the spiritual level. For example, if you are wondering whether to pursue a new path in life, you might overhear somebody mention your name and give an instruction to go ahead because the road is all clear – only to find out that the person is a stranger who's talking to somebody else. You may consider this as the response to your query. But of course, you still need to balance your otherworldly insights with common sense.

The following are the major life lessons you need to learn to help your third eye chakra blossom:

Increase your self-awareness and self-acceptance

Issues will cloud and block the third eye. This is why opening the third eye often involves dealing with your personal problems. Reflect on yourself and determine the parts that you are at odds with. Improve your understanding of yourself. This might take some time – do not be impatient with this, but consider this as part of your psychic growth. Try your best to resolve these problems so you can move on to working at higher planes. Seek a balance of different aspects of yourself – this is one of the secrets to attaining enlightenment, which encourages psychic abilities to unfold.

See yourself as part of a greater whole

In the spiritual realm, everyone and everything is one and the same. By living in accordance to this, you will lower the barriers that separate you from the rest of the universe. This implies that you will need to be more tolerant and understanding of other people and their situations. However, the reward will be great – you will perceive reality more clearly than you did before. You will no longer be distracted by your own projections about the world around you. You will also be able to tune in to the frequency that binds everything.

Application

Use your third eye – this is the best way to awaken it. We are all born with a third eye, but it weakens when we do not use it or when we ignore its messages. This is very important; don't fall into the trap of reading all there is to read about the third eye but fail to actually use it in daily life. You will exercise your third eye not with knowledge alone but with actual practice.

Chapter 10 - Different Skills the Third Eye Helps With

The third eye is your organ for perceiving beyond what the normal senses do. It's not limited to visions alone, but may include other sensory impressions such as sounds, tastes, smells, and feelings (emotional and physical sensations). It can also come as a concrete thought or as an abstract knowing about something.

Think about the third eye as an information receiver, processor, and transmitter. It can give your normal perceptions an additional layer of meaning. Just as there are many uses for the normal senses, you can also apply your sixth sense in numerous ways:

Aura Viewing

An aura is an energy field that emanates from a living creature or object. Aura viewing usually applies to reading people's auras.

The characteristics of a person's aura are affected by many things about him/her, such as his/her mental state, emotions, personality, and health condition. Because of this, you can tell a lot about that person through their aura.

It's easiest to see the aura when it's dark. Practice seeing your own aura or another person's in a dark place. Relax. Free your mind of expectations about what you will see.

Look at your own hand with an unfocused gaze. Move it slowly. You might catch a subtle radiation from your hand. Have a partner stand in front of a blank, white wall. Gaze at the space around him/her. Keep your gaze relaxed. The kinds of images you perceive depend on your third eye's receptivity to subtle energies. Practice your ability to see faint radiations – Soon enough you will no longer need to do aura readings in the dark.

Aura reading books ascribe interpretations to aura colors and features. These may be useful for you, but for more accurate results, you must acquaint yourself with how your mind translates energies into sensory signals. Energies usually are translated differently with every perceiver. For example, one psychic will say that the person's aura is vivid yellow; another will say it's loud like thunder, while a third one might compare it to a hot flame. But they will all agree that this person has a dominant personality that others are uneasy with.

Experiment with this. It's better if you don't know the person you are reading so you won't be biased. Try to interpret what comes to you then ask the person if your interpretations are correct. Record everything so you'll have notes on where you got it right and where you need revisions. Soon enough, you'll accumulate a list of interpretations that are fairly consistent with every reading.

For example, you might keep on getting the color pastel blue if the person has a peaceful nature, or a shaky feeling if he is constantly anxious, etc. This is a painstaking procedure, but it will provide you with more satisfying results than when you base your readings on somebody else's interpretations.

As mentioned above, aura reading can be done to non-living things, even locations. You can hold an object in your hand (object reading is called psychometry) or meditate in a place (scanning the environment) to receive auric emanations from it.

Tarot

The tarot is a set of cards that can be used for various purposes: for trying to determine the possible outcomes of an action, for unearthing hidden issues that are affecting a situation, for determining the characteristics of a certain individual, etc. It basically allows you to gain information about a subject.

Tarot cards usually come with a manual that tells you how to use them. The cards have certain meanings assigned to them – although there are many varieties of tarot, the interpretations are quite similar among them. However, there are some divinatory cards that do not follow the tarot pattern.

There are three ways to read the tarot: by basing the interpretation on the meanings assigned to the card, by using your third eye, or by combining book-based interpretation and third eye perception.

Using the third eye when reading the tarot may take more energy than simply reading the manual, but it often gives more accurate insights. Using the tarot with the third eye requires you to be in a psychic state. Clear your mind and focus on the topic. Shuffle the cards. Pick some cards and arrange them according to your desired tarot spread (tarot spreads are card arrangements – there are popular tarot spreads but you can also make your own spread).

Look at the card. Close your eyes and wait for visions, sounds, and other perception to come into your head. You can either list these down or record them. Do not interpret them as of now. Simply let them arrive. Interpretation requires beta wave thinking, which will push you out of the psychic state.

You can also interact with the card. Tarot cards are said to be doorways to the astral plane. Visualize the card as a door that you can walk in and out from. Observe what's in the tarot because what you experience might answer your question. You can also talk to the character/s in the card.

When you're done with each card, combine all the insights into a narrative. Write down notes about the reading as well – include the date and the issue of the reading. Go back to your notes when a particular issue is resolved or when an outcome has arrived, and see whether your reading made sense.

Other divinatory tools such as the I-Ching, the Runes, Geomancy, and Tea Leaves also have their own traditionally ascribed interpretations. If you learn these techniques, you can use your knowledge of the method in conjunction with your third eye impressions to get the best results.

Dowsing

Dowsing is a divination skill that makes use of tools such as a pendulum or dowsing rods. These dowsing tools do not have an inherent magical ability in themselves, but they move in response to your own body's automatic movements. When your third eye is awakened, your physical body will be able to sense emanations from the other planes. This will enable your muscles to send signals to answer what you want to know.

Using a Dowsing rod

The dowsing rod is traditionally used to locate water sources or buried objects. It theoretically works not because of the dowsing rods but because of the dowser's sensitivity to electromagnetic fields. Once your third eye is awakened, you will also increase your ability to detect these fields, but it will take trial and error to interpret these signals reliably.

You can buy dowsing rods in a store selling occult supplies or new age shops, but you can also simply bend two wires into L-shapes. You hold the short edge of the L in each hand while letting the longer edge stick out away from you. Move around the location – if the two edges overlap, it means that you are hitting your target.

Pendulum Dowsing

A pendulum is a small object that is suspended on a string or chain. This is held in one hand and allowed to move freely. The pendulum's movements are assigned a meaning: for example, clockwise means yes, counterclockwise means no, sideways means maybe, and up and down means a refusal to answer the question. You can choose your own interpretations. Before the dowsing session, move the pendulum and say out loud what the particular movement means. This 'programs' the pendulum into responding in the ways you assign it to.

You can also make charts for pendulums. Write the pendulum options: say, days of the week, a list of remedies, a collection of names, etc. Put a dot in the middle of the paper. Make a semi-circle with the dot at the center of the base. Cut this semi-circle into evenly spaced divisions fanning out from the center – the number of options will determine the number of divisions. Write down the options within the spaces between the lines. To use the pendulum chart, position the pendulum on top of the center dot, ask your question, and let it swing freely. The direction it goes to gives your reply.

Telepathy

Telepathy is connecting to another person's mind. Some experts recommend practicing with somebody you are comfortable with – this makes sense because you already have a connection and it will be easier to discuss the things that you perceive. On the other hand, your knowledge of the person may bias what you perceive from him/her. But practically, it will be more awkward to practice telepathy with a stranger rather than a friend, so start with a buddy.

Sending and receiving images

Thoughts are rather complex, so it's best to begin with something simple like an image. Decide who between you and your partner will be the sender and receiver. Let the sender think about one or more images, and have him/her draw these on a piece of paper. Afterwards, the person will send the image/s telepathically. At the same time, the receiver will connect with the sender. You can just intend the message to be received or sent, or visualize a tube connecting your heads. The receiver will list down what is perceived, and when it's done, the two of you will compare notes.

Sending and receiving emotions

Emotions are another example of an easy telepathy target because the subconscious mind (the psychic part of the mind) deals with emotions. The sender will spend a few minutes generating a strong feeling in themselves. This can be done by recalling experiences when the emotion occurred, imagining scenarios that provoke the feeling, or by visualizing concepts associated with it (example, darkness, scary noises, and running people can be linked with fear). The receiver will clear his/her mind and heart and wait until he/she feels something. To help with the connection, the sender and receiver may imagine a tube connecting their hearts. The receiver will say what he/she received and guess the emotion.

Sending and receiving instructions

This is more advanced than the previous two because the mind doesn't want to be told what to do, especially if the command comes from another person. The receiver should be in an ultra-receptive state of mind so that the sender can pass on the instruction. This can be done in three ways:

1. The sender can talk to the receiver telepathically

2. The sender can imagine the receiver doing the instruction

3. The sender can do the instruction in his/her own mind and then pass on the experience to the receiver (example, the sender wants the receiver to scratch his/her nose; he/she will scratch his/her own nose mentally then imagine the experience transferring into the receiver)

For practical reasons, a time limit should be set to allow the receiver to perform the instruction. However, it's possible that the instruction will be done outside of the time limit.

Talking to Spirit Guides

Spirit guides are beings that assist people. They can be various entities such as angels, elementals, fairies, aliens, departed relatives, famous people, archetypes, and so on. The spirit guide could also be the universe itself – it is said that the universe is conscious and anyone receptive enough can tap into its wisdom.

There are detailed instructions for meeting spirit guides. Some entities require rituals – such as when you are calling on a spirit from a magickal grimoire. Basically though, you just prepare yourself for meeting the guide by finding a place where you can make contact. If you want to talk with a water elemental for example, you may go to a beach.

It could happen entirely in your head though. Create with your imagination an area where you will interact with your guide. Invite the guide to come to you and say your intentions. Wait for a response. Remember that the spirits have their own ways of communicating with us. Do not force them to talk with you in a particular way – such as forcing them to appear in concrete form or talk in a loud and clear voice. Instead, open your mind to whatever may arrive and record it. You may find that the messages make sense later on.

The Third Eye Simply Explained

The third eye is a part of the person that enables him/her to access and send information in special ways. It consists not only of the sense of sight, but of all the senses plus your thoughts. It perceives much more than what the ordinary consciousness is used to paying attention to. It can process information in dynamic ways and can reveal patterns that your ordinary mind might miss.

Some Uses of the Third Eye

- Answer questions

- Understand connections

- Gather information

- Feel energies

- Manipulate energies

You will find plenty of other uses for your third eye the more that you use it and the more you become immersed in the world of the occult and paranormal. Take note that using psychic energy requires life force – you might get tired if you use the third eye often. This is the reason why psychics tend to lose their accuracy when they are tested continuously.

Do not strain yourself. If you notice that you are missing instead of hitting, take a break. Resume when you are feeling better. If you are having trouble with a particular issue because you are too affected by it, ask another psychic to help you. Also, consider engaging in energy-enhancing practices such as yoga, exercise, meditation, etc. to make it easier for you to function psychically without being drained.

The most important thing when using your psychic abilities is to get into the psychic state of mind. This prevents you from interfering with your psychic impressions. Your fears, expectations, concerns, desires, and biases will color what you receive from your third eye so you should do your absolute best to be as relaxed and unattached as possible.

Chapter 11:
The Third Eye & Brainwave Levels

Activating the third eye involves brainwave level changes. This reflects the changes of mental states.

Brain cells produce electricity, which takes on various patterns and rhythms, which are measured in cycles per second or Hertz (Hz). Humans have certain types of electrical patterns occurring in the brain – these are called brain waves. These brain waves can be observed with the use of an EEG (electroencephalograph). Each kind of brain wave becomes dominant during certain situations to serve specific purposes.

The brain's ability to switch through different brain wave frequencies determines our ability to do various tasks such as to handle stress, concentrate, relax, store or retrieve memories, and get the most out of sleep. This is why no single brainwave is better than the rest. However, with regards to psychic ability, the brainwaves that are ideal for it are alpha, theta, and sometimes delta – as observed from the EEG readings of people performing psychic feats.

There are five basic brainwaves that are known so far:

Gamma (40 Hz – 100 Hz)

This brainwave type has the highest frequency among the four. This occurs when there is an excess of sensory stimulation. It accompanies a heightened focus. Intense meditation may produce gamma brain waves. Meditating yogis and monks who have performed incredible feats such as heating wet towels with their own bodies were said to have a surplus of gamma waves in their ECG readings.

An overproduction of gamma waves can lead to feeling overwhelmed and stressed. Underproduction can mean learning impairments and mood disorders. A safe way to increase gamma waves is through meditation.

Beta (12 Hz – 40 Hz)

The beta brainwave is the state of mind that we are most used to. It is the normal mental state we are in when we do our daily activities. We are in beta when we work, read, write, solve problems rationally, socialize, talk with others, and focus on something. This brainwave type allows us to concentrate on our tasks and to think logically. It is the alert state – the realm of the chattering mind.

Beta is not really good for operating psychically. Impressions attained at this state are usually projections of the mind and not the perception of the third eye.

An excess of beta waves causes restlessness and stress. A low amount of beta waves when they are needed result in a lack of focus or ADHD symptoms. Being busy with something tends to increase beta waves. Other than that, taking stimulants such as coffee and energy drinks will also do the trick.

Alpha (8Hz – 12 Hz)

This is the middle zone between the conscious and subconscious mind. This brainwave enables easy recall of memories and creative thought. Alpha waves accompany a relaxed state of mind, such as during reflecting, daydreaming, fantasizing, and imagining.

Alpha waves are very conducive for psychic functioning. Psychics often go into alpha so they can use their third eye.

High levels of alpha brainwaves can cause one to lose focus or become too relaxed, and daydreams may occur. Low levels may cause sleeplessness, OCD, and anxiety. To increase alpha waves, you can relax and close your eyes or take a substance (not recommended) that causes relaxation such as alcohol or marijuana.

Theta (4 Hz – 8 Hz)

Theta brainwaves characterize the subconscious mind. Theta is linked with emotions, particularly strong ones. These brainwaves enable you to connect with emotions and with deep-seated memories. This may improve intuition and creativity as well.

The theta state is the state of suggestibility. This is where your mind lowers its defenses and accepts suggestions without resisting. Hypnotists make their clients go into theta. You can also practice self-hypnosis (such as using affirmations) on yourself when you're at this level.

Theta brainwaves are also common among psychics who are using their abilities. Being inactive, dreaming, or sleeping can cause a person to reach the theta level.

A surplus of theta waves can cause intense emotionality, while a lack of these can cause one to feel numb or have low emotional awareness. Increasing theta waves may be done by deeply relaxing and by sleeping.

Delta (0 Hz – 4 Hz)

The delta state is where the deepest and most productive sleep occurs. Delta waves are said to be involved in automatic bodily functions. This is the best time for the cells of the body to be regenerated and for the immune system to fight illnesses. The delta state may also enable psychic abilities such as astral projection and out of body experiences.

An abnormally large number of delta waves can mean brain disorders and severe ADHD. A small number of these when they're expected is associated with the inability to refresh the body and mind, as well as a poor quality of sleep. Increasing delta waves is possible by going into a deep and undisturbed sleep.

How to Change Brainwave Levels to Enter the Psychic State

Ordinary functioning involves beta brainwaves. This is what we are used to when we go about our daily activities. This is where logical and linear thought occurs.

Using the third eye involves using a state of mind that's different from what we normally use. Before we can use our third eye, we must bring ourselves out of the normal state of mind (Beta) and enter a psychic trance.

Signs of psychic trance

- Slowed breathing and heart rate
- Possible increase in body temperature, you may sweat
- Passiveness – physical and mental
- Visions seen while eyes are closed
- Eyes may automatically move such as during REM (rapid eye movement) sleep/dreams
- Increase of galvanic skin resistance (skin electricity)

- Body may sway slightly

These are the two general methods for how this can be achieved:

Over-arousal

- Chanting
- Rapid dancing
- Hyperventilation
- Frantic body movements
- Music
- Drugs

Under-arousal

- Relaxation (physical, emotional, and mental relaxation)
- Meditation
- Slow breathing
- Blanking the mind
- Focusing your attention
- Self-hypnosis
- Visualization exercises
- Dream control (research Lucid Dreaming for more info)

Under-arousal is the safer and more commonly used method in achieving a psychic trance state. You can access your awakened third eye simply by closing your eyes, relaxing your body, and clearing your thoughts to let information stream in.

Conclusion

Awakening the sixth sense may be difficult, and may require you a lot of effort, but in the end, it will reward you with psychic powers and abilities. It is, however, important that upon receiving these gifts, one uses them wisely and for the good of other people.

Thank you again for downloading this book!

I hope this book was able to help you learn more about third eye awakening and what it means!

The next step is to put this information to use, and begin working on your third eye and psychic abilities!

Also don't forget to download my **FREE** report on the 7 Keys for Successful Meditation by following the link - http://bit.ly/1F91lfl

Finally, if you enjoyed this book, please take the time to share your thoughts and post a review on Amazon. It'd be greatly appreciated!

Thank you and good luck!

www.ingramcontent.com/pod-product-compliance
Lightning Source LLC
LaVergne TN
LVHW021740060526
838200LV00052B/3377